TO LIVE IS

CHRIST

DAY BY DAY

BETH MOORE

B&H
PUBLISHING GROUP

NASHVILLE, TENNESSEE

I give thanks to my God for every
remembrance of you, always praying
with joy for all of you in my every prayer,
because of your partnership in the gospel
from the first day until now. I am sure of
this, that he who started a good work in
you will carry it on to completion until
the day of Christ Jesus. . . .

My eager expectation and hope is that
I will not be ashamed about anything,
but that now as always, with all boldness,
Christ will be highly honored in my
body, whether by life or by death. For me,
living is Christ and dying is gain.

Philippians 1:3–6, 20–21

"Who are You, Lord?" he said. "I am Jesus, whom you are persecuting," He replied.
   —Acts 9:5–6

∽

Long after Jesus interrupted Paul's plans on the road to Damascus, the apostle's account of that event remained constant. Something dramatically changed the life of a brilliantly devious persecutor.

I pray that the same Someone who encountered Paul will also interrupt your life with His glorious presence as you journey through this book.

Paul's writings embody a passion for Christ that is unparalleled in the New Testament. I have accepted many of his words as a personal challenge. "I want to know Christ" has become my plea.

"To live is Christ and to die is gain" has become my hope. I am a fan of all those past and present who have loved Him with their whole lives, as Paul did.

May these pages enhance your love and devotion for Christ so dramatically that He is indeed freed in your life to do more than your eyes have seen, more than your ears have heard, and more than your mind has conceived.

"To live is Christ!" When you can say these words and mean them, you have discovered life at its fullest.

∾

I will never boast about anything except the cross of our Lord Jesus Christ, through whom the world has been crucified to me.
   —*Galatians 6:14*

Bind them as a sign on your hand and let
them be a symbol on your forehead.
    —Deuteronomy 6:8

∾

By the time Saul was thirteen years of
age, he was considered a son of the law,
assuming all the religious responsibilities
of the adult Jew.

He started wearing phylacteries, called
tefillin, during weekday morning prayers.
Phylacteries were made up of two black
leather cubes with long leather straps.
Each cube held certain passages from the
Torah written on strips of parchment.
Saul wore one of the cubes on his left arm
facing his heart. The other cube was
placed in the center of his forehead. The
leather straps on the left arm were wound
precisely seven times around his arm.

The left arm was chosen because it was ordinarily the weaker. Jews were to wear God's Word as a banner and shield over their weakness. You see, a thirteen-year-old Hebrew boy could not even get out of bed in the morning without remembering to whom he belonged. The law of the Lord was his life.

We don't practice the outward expression of the Jew, but we are wise to share the inward principle. May we keep ourselves continually in God's Word, and may He keep His Word continually in us.

ᔪ

Your word is a lamp for my feet and a light on my path. I have solemnly sworn to keep Your righteous judgments.
    —Psalm 119:105–106

*Everything is from God, who reconciled
us to Himself through Christ and gave us
the ministry of reconciliation.*
  —2 Corinthians 5:18

∽

On Saul's first visit to Jerusalem as a
thirteen-year-old boy, he probably ran up
the main street to the house of the Lord.
He surely conjured up pictures of King
David dancing down that very street.
He hurried up the many stairs to greet
magnificent porches surrounding the
entire enclosure.

Then he walked to a wall, one that held
tremendous significance for the Jew, but
one that would hold far more significance for a Jew who would ultimately
become the world's most renowned
missionary to the Gentiles.

When from a prison cell in Ephesus, Paul wrote that Christ had broken down the wall that separates Jew and Gentile, the apostle was not simply referring to a figurative wall of partition. He was referring to an imposing structure he had faced on the temple grounds as an adolescent many years before. This literal wall of partition in the temple forbade access of the defiling heathen into the inner sanctuaries of the house of God.

What different emotions he would feel later as he came to despise the prejudice of those who would not recognize the walls crumbled by the cross.

〰

He is our peace, who made both groups one and tore down the dividing wall of hostility.
    —Ephesians 2:14

*As for you, continue in what you have
learned and firmly believed, knowing those
from whom you learned.*
   —2 Timothy 3:14

∿

One of the most wonderful concepts in
the Word of God concerns the plan He
has for our lives. In Galatians 1:15, Paul
described God as the One "who from my
mother's womb set me apart and called
me by His grace." Yes, God had a plan for
Saul from birth. Nothing in the young
man's life would be a waste unless he
refused to let God use it.

In hindsight, then, it's no wonder that
Saul took a seat in the classroom of the
rabbi Gamaliel, grandson of the great
Hillel—names of considerable impor-
tance in the history of Judaism.

All of Saul's religious training, his countless hours spent in Scripture and study, and his brilliance in spiritual matters would all be parts of God's ornate plan. God would use what Saul learned at the feet of Gamaliel, one of Judaism's most grace-filled teachers, one who was so highly revered that the Jews referred to him as "the beauty of the law."

God in His wonderful wisdom made sure that the law was taught to Saul with a touch of rare grace. He has gone ahead of you, too, to prepare you for the plans He's established for your life.

∽

We are His creation—created in Christ Jesus for good works, which God prepared ahead of time so that we should walk in them.
   —Ephesians 2:10

Keep Your servant from willful sins; do not let
them rule over me. Then I will be innocent,
and cleansed from blatant rebellion.
   —Psalm 19:13

∾

Many of the Pharisees and members of
the Sanhedrin whom Christ encountered
were Saul's instructors or classmates.
The term *Pharisee* was meant to represent
genuine piety and deep devotion to God.
Although exceptions certainly existed
among the Pharisees, the term in the days
of Jesus and Saul had become synonymous with hypocrisy and cynicism.

Matthew 23 is an entire discourse
addressed to the teachers of the law and
Pharisees. In reading it, notice all the
specific ways Jesus described the same
people Saul encountered in Jerusalem.

For example, they made demands of others that they themselves did not keep (v. 4); they made their religious actions into show to impress others (v. 5); they loved to be the center of attention (v. 6); and they not only wouldn't enter the kingdom of God, they prevented others from entering (v. 13).

Do any of these describe you as well? Godly people are valiant people. They are people with the courage to ask God to spotlight areas of weakness, sin, and failure. Then God can strengthen, heal, and complete what is lacking.

∽

May the words of my mouth and the meditation of my heart be acceptable to You, LORD, my rock and my Redeemer.
    —Psalm 19:14

As to the law, a Pharisee; as to zeal, persecuting the church; as to the righteousness that is in the law, blameless.
   —Philippians 3:5–6

∽

We cannot begin to comprehend what Saul's life was like as he sought to orient his actions by the letter of the law. Daily rituals determined the first words out of his mouth in the morning, the way he took off his nightclothes and put on his day clothes, and how he sprinkled his hands before breakfast. He carefully avoided eating or drinking quickly and never ate while standing. He pronounced numerous benedictions through the day.

So do you get the general idea of what Saul's life was like as he attempted to live by the law "blamelessly"?

Saul was strangled by the letter of the law. He tried desperately to keep the outward acts of obedience while his heart slowly eroded. Inevitably, Saul's faraway heart would turn to faraway actions. Without love for God and His Word, we're just trying to be good. Nothing will wear us out faster.

Oh, God, forgive us when we act like modern-day Pharisees. Convict us at the very moment of our departure from the law of love You have written on our hearts. Give us hearts of devotion, not heads full of religion.

∽

These people approach Me with their mouths to honor Me with lip-service—yet their hearts are far from Me.
    —Isaiah 29:13

*Some from Cilicia and Asia came forward
and disputed with Stephen. But they were
unable to stand up against the wisdom and
the Spirit by whom he spoke.*
   —Acts 6:9–10

∽

As the months passed following Jesus'
resurrection, the number of His followers
grew, as did their boldness. Saul was
disgusted over the way the Pharisees had
mishandled this problem. So he packed
his things and headed for Jerusalem,
salivating for the chance to be the hero.

Saul arrived in Jerusalem just in time to
hear an infuriating speech from a man
named Stephen, who had been sentenced
to death by stoning, based on some false
charges they had cooked up against him,
just as they had done with Jesus.

While they were stoning him, Stephen cried out, "Lord, do not charge them with this sin!" (Acts 7:60). These words were to have a permanent impact on Saul. The seed may have taken a while to germinate, but the rabbi from Tarsus would never escape the witness of Stephen.

When I get to heaven, I know I want first to see my Savior. But when I've spent a few centuries at His feet, I'd like to take a basin and a towel to wash the feet of those who have meant so much to me here. I think Stephen has a high place on the "wash list" of Saul of Tarsus.

＊

In Him we have redemption through His blood, the forgiveness of our trespasses, according to the riches of His grace.
   —Ephesians 1:7

They threw him out of the city and began to
stone him. And the witnesses laid their robes
at the feet of a young man named Saul.
   —Acts 7:58

∽

Yes, Saul was there, giving approval to
Stephen's death. The original Greek word
for *approval* means "to take pleasure with
others." It is a word sometimes used of
both parties in a marriage who are
mutually pleased with something.

Applying the original meaning to Saul's
actions, the scene becomes clearer. He
was pleased with their actions, and they
were pleased with his approval. A mutual
admiration society, enjoying everything.
Saul didn't just give his approval when
Stephen breathed his last. He cheered at
every blow, like points on a scoreboard.

As Jesus watched, He didn't miss a single nod of Saul's phylacteried head. Can you imagine the alloy of emotions He must have experienced as He looked on these two key players in the kingdom that day?

One *for* Him; one *against* Him. One covered in blood; the other covered by prayer shawls. One who could not save himself from men; the other who could not save himself from sin. One dead in body but alive in spirit; the other alive in body but dead in spirit. One loved by God; and the other loved by God.

Grace, grace, God's grace.

∽

Blessed is the man who does not condemn himself by what he approves.
    —Romans 14:22

As he traveled and was nearing Damascus,
a light from heaven suddenly flashed around
him. Falling to the ground, he heard a voice
saying to him, "Saul, Saul, why are you
persecuting Me?"
  —Acts 9:3–4

∽

I can see young Saul strutting around
Jerusalem, determined to make a name
for himself as a hotheaded rabbi seeking
authorization to arrest followers of Jesus
in Damascus. He was on this journey
when God intervened and knocked him
off his donkey.

Would you agree that no example could
much better illustrate the statement that
a person can be sincere in his beliefs yet
be sincerely wrong? Saul knew it all, and
yet he knew nothing.

I used to see everything in black and white. I've concluded that for those who only see gray, God often emphatically and lovingly paints portraits of black and white so they are forced to acknowledge the contrasts. For those who only see black and white, He introduces situations when answers aren't so easy, where lists "A to Z" cannot be found, and when points one, two, and three don't work.

Some things are gray such as, "Why did He choose us?" But some things are still black and white—I once was lost, but now I'm found, was blind but now I see.

∾

If anyone among you thinks he is wise in this age, he must become foolish so that he can become wise.
  —*1 Corinthians 3:18*

*"Christ Jesus came into the world to save
sinners"*—and I am the worst of them.
   —1 Timothy 1:15

∽

In Saul's dramatic conversion, you and
I get to see the evil of a sinner's heart.

I'm certainly no counselor, but I suspect
that most obsessions rise from a futile
attempt to fill a gaping hole somewhere
deep in a life. Saul's external righteousness and achieved goals left behind an
itch he could not scratch. Can you
imagine how miserable he must have
been? Religiously righteous to the bone,
inside he had nothing but innately
wicked marrow. All that work, and it
hadn't worked. All his righteous passion
turned into unrighteous zeal, and he
became dangerous.

But we also get to see the purity of a Savior's mercy. Christ met Saul on the path to his darkest, most devious sin. For this very moment, for the depths of Saul's depravity, Christ had already died. Christ literally caught him in the act.

Jesus sent Saul to open the eyes of many and turn them from darkness to light so they could receive forgiveness of sins. No greater calling exists, as well as no room for pride. God's servant was never more than a flashback from humility. No one can teach forgiveness like the forgiven.

∿

Indeed, the Lord's *hand is not too short to save, and His ear is not too deaf to hear. But your iniquities have built barriers between you and your God.*
—Isaiah 59:1–2

*All who heard him were astounded and said,
"Isn't this the man who, in Jerusalem, was
destroying those who called on this name?"*
   —Acts 9:21

∽

Few things are more precious than the
expressions on a newborn's face as he or
she is suddenly cast from the darkness of
the womb into the bright lights of the
delivery room. I remember both laugh-
ing and crying at my daughters' faces
screwing up indignantly as if to say,
"Would the same wise guy who turned
on that light mind turning it off?"

Many years ago when a grown man was
born again on a dusty road to Damascus,
a light came on that no one was able to
turn off. We will soon discover many
who tried.

Saul was hardly the kind of man to be ignored. Saul with the gospel was like a teenager with the radio. He kept turning up the volume. Inevitably, ironically, the Jews in Damascus conspired to kill him, so Saul took the first basket out of town.

Can you imagine how differently Saul must have approached Jerusalem this time? Every step had new significance. He walked through the city gates where his face was recognized instantly. The chief priests expected him to return with prisoners. Instead, only one prisoner returned: a prisoner of Jesus Christ.

∽

You have put off the old man with his practices and have put on the new man.
  —Colossians 3:9–10

Barnabas, however, took him and brought him to the apostles.
   —Acts 9:27

∾

God had issued Saul an undeniable apostolic calling. He probably assumed his place was with the other apostles. But when he arrived in Jerusalem and tried to associate with them, "they were all afraid of him, since they did not believe he was a disciple" (Acts 9:26).

Two wonderful words begin the next verse: "But Barnabas." Without a doubt Barnabas was a hero. Few things touch my heart more than Christian men who risk vulnerability in obedience to Christ. Barnabas reached out a helping hand to a discouraged man. Saul took that hand. Two lives bonded in that moment.

God used Barnabas to give others the courage to be the people He had called them to be. When Barnabas brought Saul before the other apostles, they may have remembered how each of them had been the focus of his encouragement at one time or another. Now he encouraged them to accept a new brother.

Many probably criticized Barnabas for being gullible concerning Saul. Barnabas was willing to give people a chance even when others weren't. Let's look for ways to be a Barnabas in another's life.

ॐ

I have great joy and encouragement from your love, because the hearts of the saints have been refreshed through you.
   —Philemon 7

"You know it's forbidden for a Jewish man to associate with or visit a foreigner. But God has shown me that I must not call any person common or unclean."
—Acts 10:28

∽

One of the main differences between Peter and Paul (Saul) was the contrast in their callings. Peter was entrusted with the Jews; Saul, with the Gentiles.

I suspect that Peter often thought of Saul's calling and was relieved it wasn't his! Imagine how many times he thought of Saul's being called to minister to the Gentiles and said, "Better him than me!" Saul might as well have been called to lepers. Peter may have even wondered if Saul's punishment for persecuting the church was to get the leftovers.

His attitude is nothing new. Many otherwise strong, God-serving, Bible-believing Christians have been steeped in prejudice from birth. We are challenged to overcome prejudice on many levels. Differences will always exist, but division doesn't always have to result. We must be careful to avoid spiritual elitism.

Everything we are and anything we possess as believers in Christ is a gift of grace. We must aggressively fight the enemy when he seeks to nullify our growth and good works by making them invitations for pride and prejudice.

If you show favoritism, you commit sin and are convicted by the law as transgressors.
  —James 2:9

*I faced dangers from rivers, dangers
from robbers, dangers from my own people,
dangers from the Gentiles, dangers in the
city, dangers in the open country.*
　—2 Corinthians 11:26

∽

After the Grecian Jews tried to kill him in
Jerusalem, Saul boarded a boat for Tarsus,
his homeland. Five years passed between
this departure to Tarsus and his next
appearance in Scripture. Many scholars
refer to these as the "missing years."

But consider a few things that might
have happened to him during this
interim period. The Lord told Ananias
that He would show Saul how much he
must suffer for His name. I believe God
began fulfilling this prophecy almost
immediately.

Figuratively speaking, he was thrown into many fires during his ministry, yet few would have been any hotter than those in Tarsus. He was the local hero among the Jewish community there. Most people knew he had left Tarsus years earlier for the express purpose of dealing with the followers of the Way. Now he returned as one of them. I doubt anyone threw him a homecoming party.

Have you been through seasons when it felt like the floodgates were open, when trouble was coming from all directions? What do you think God expects of us in times like these?

∽

Now for a short time you have had to be distressed by various trials.
—*1 Peter 1:6*

And the disciples were first called Christians in Antioch.
   —Acts 11:26

∾

What a great word: *Christian*—
an emotional word causing one man joy
and another man fury, causing one man
peace and another man turmoil.

A dividing word unceasingly drawing a
line. Either a man *is* or he is not; he is
either for or against.

A uniting word, drawing together
unlikely pairs in workplaces and
neighborhoods over one single bond.

A defining word for which countless
people have lived and countless people
have died.

Christian was a label coined by unbelievers as a form of ridicule. How beautifully God stole the victory from Satan. The very word used as a mockery became the greatest privilege a man could boast.

Two thousand years after a man called Jesus of Nazareth walked the streets of Jerusalem, two billion people alive on this earth today call themselves by the ever-dividing, ever-uniting word— *Christian*. God is still scattering the seeds a few righteous renegades planted in a city called Antioch. Had they only known what they were starting.

ം

If anyone suffers as a Christian, he should not be ashamed, but should glorify God with that name.
   —1 Peter 4:16

As they were ministering to the Lord and fasting, the Holy Spirit said, "Set apart for Me Barnabas and Saul for the work that I have called them to."
  —Acts 13:2

∽

The Holy Spirit instructed the church in Antioch to send Barnabas and Saul on a mission to other cities and regions, spreading the good news into uncharted Christian territory.

Again and again in Scripture we see God's perfect timing. In Galatians 1:15, the apostle explains that he was set apart from birth (about AD 10). He did not receive salvation until around AD 36. He was not set apart for his signature ministry until around AD 46, commissioned by the church in Antioch.

Yet not one minute was wasted. God was training Saul during those formative years. When God's time came, Saul and Barnabas were ready for the Holy Spirit to send them out.

This moment is so precious to me. Meet the first international missionaries: Saul and Barnabas! Set apart to be sent off—just like so many other faithful ones who have followed in their footsteps, forsaking the securities of home and family to follow Christ anywhere. I have no greater admiration for any group of people.

∾

My righteousness is near, My salvation appears, and My arms will bring justice to the nations.
    —Isaiah 51:5

I have written these things to you about those who are trying to deceive you.
    —1 John 2:26

ᔓ

Saul (whose name had been changed to Paul) got no farther than the second stop on his first missionary journey when he met a man I'm sure he never forgot. His name was Bar-Jesus (or Elymas).

Bar-Jesus did everything he could to oppose Paul and Barnabas and to keep the proconsul from believing their message. Paul rebuked this sorcerer, and God struck him blind. Paul called him a "son of the Devil" (Acts 13:10). He was actually using a play on words because the name Bar-Jesus in Aramaic means "son of Jesus." In effect, Paul was saying, "You're no son of Jesus. You're a son of the devil!"

Think of times you've picked up your Bible and were interrupted, distracted. How often when you attend a worship service are you distracted while preparing to go, on the way, or at the service? Does your annoyance turn into anger directed at a child, spouse, or friend? Our anger needs to be directed at the source.

When you desire to study God's Word, Satan will do everything to distract. Ask the Holy Spirit to empower you to recognize the source of your distractions and to channel your anger where it belongs—toward the evil one.

∽

The great dragon was thrown out—the ancient serpent, who is called the Devil and Satan, the one who deceives the whole world.
    —Revelation 12:9

*The leaders of the synagogue sent word
to them, saying, "Brothers, if you have any
message of encouragement for the people,
you can speak."*
  —Acts 13:15

∽

Sometimes we yearn for God to crack
open a receptive door to share our faith.
We scramble to grab an opportunity that
never seems to come. Other times God
swings open a door so quickly, we're too
stunned to walk through it!

God swung the door open so quickly in
Pisidian Antioch that He almost blew the
beard off the rabbi! Practically by the
time Paul and Barnabas found a chair,
they were asked to share a message of
encouragement. Paul was not about to
miss a golden opportunity.

Like any good orator, he shaped his style
and material to fit his audience. As he
stood in the synagogue, he addressed
Jews and those who believed in the God
of Israel. He presented the gospel by
rehearsing for them their history. He
urged them to see how perfectly Christ
knit the past with the present. They did
not have to forsake their history. They
just needed to accept the rest of the story!

What glorious news! If a person who had
shared the responsibility for Christ's
death could be forgiven, can any person
be beyond forgiveness?

∾

*I am not ashamed of the gospel, because
it is God's power for salvation to everyone
who believes.*
    —Romans 1:16

*The Jews incited the religious women of high
standing and the leading men of the city.
They stirred up persecution against Paul
and Barnabas and expelled them from
their district.*

   —Acts 13:50

〜

This group of ancient Jews had been
privileged to receive the ministry of Paul,
but in a flash they went from being
subjects of ministry to being sources of
opposition, inciting other men and
women of influence to give additional
weight and volume to their criticism.

Little has changed. Satan still takes
advantage of us, hoping to seize our
powers of influence for his own purposes.
Think of ways you exert the power of
influence, whether rightly or wrongly.

You're probably more influential than you thought. If you had lunch with friends this week, you probably influenced someone in some way. If a friend shared a problem with you, you influenced him or her somehow with your response. If you gave your opinion on a matter recently, you very likely affected someone else's.

We are constantly exerting influence. Influence is a gift, a trust. We must be careful how we use it. Take heed. Satan can affect masses of followers through a few leaders.

∽

A righteous man is careful in dealing with his neighbor, but the ways of wicked men lead them astray.
    —Proverbs 12:26

When an attempt was made by both
the Gentiles and Jews, with their rulers,
to assault and stone them, they found out
about it and fled.
—Acts 14:5–6

∽

Shouldn't Paul and Barnabas have chosen
to stay, trusting God to guard them from
attack since they were doing His will and
preaching His message? Couldn't the
same power used to perform signs and
miracles be used to stifle their enemies?
Instead they ran for their lives!

I believe their actions offer us a fitting
description of this dynamic duo: they
were smart! I don't believe they were
reacting out of pure fear. They were
responding out of pure wisdom—
and quickly!

Christ *did* deliver Paul and Barnabas from an evil attack. He just used their heads and feet to do it!

Whether God uses natural means or supernatural means to deliver us from danger, both are divine provisions. God supplied the healthy legs that Paul and Barnabas used to flee. God provides the car we drive to the nearest public place when we're being followed. The person who walks onto the scene out of nowhere and frightens off an attacker is an ambassador of God! Thank God for His natural forms of provision!

∽

A sensible person sees danger and takes cover, but the inexperienced keep going and are punished.
   —Proverbs 22:3

When the crowds saw what Paul had done,
they raised their voices, saying . . . "The gods
have come down to us in the form of men!"
  —Acts 14:11

∽

Paul and Barnabas not only tore their clothes in grief when the people made such a preposterous assumption, but they wasted no time in setting the record straight. They did not capitalize on a moment's glory. They did not use others' attentions to get a home-cooked meal.

We all know that human beings are indescribably fickle. One minute we are laying palm branches in the road and crying, "Hosanna in the highest." The next minute we're crying, "Crucify Him," or, "I never knew Him." That's how it went with this adoring crowd.

One minute they were preparing to worship Paul and Barnabas. "Then some Jews came from Antioch and Iconium, and when they had won over the crowds and stoned Paul, they dragged him out of the city, thinking he was dead" (v. 19).

That didn't take long, did it? Paul and Barnabas could have slipped out of town without a scratch. Instead, Paul was stoned so severely that they dragged him outside the city thinking he was dead.

How do you handle compliments and success? What happens when we depend on others' opinions to feed our pride?

∽

He did not need anyone to testify about man; for He Himself knew what was in man.
   —John 2:25

"It is necessary to pass through many troubles on our way into the kingdom of God."
—Acts 14:22

～

We may not find a message about unavoidable troubles very strengthening! But *fear* of trials sometimes depletes more energy than *facing* trials! Once we accept the inevitability of hardship, we can begin to redirect our focus from fear of trials to faithfulness. In the face of tribulations, we often sense a heavenly strength filling our souls right on time.

Realizing the inevitability of hardship encourages us in the faith. I would be pretty discouraged if I thought hardships in the lives of surrendered Christians were unusual and were always signs of disobedience.

We are usually aware when consequences of sin have caused us deep suffering, but many other times trials have nothing at all to do with disobedience. Believing a heretical prosperity gospel can leave us terribly discouraged, wondering what we've done wrong. We wonder why we can't seem to muster enough faith to be healthy, problem free, and prosperous.

Know that difficulty is not a sure sign of immaturity or faithlessness. The Spirit will do His job and let you know if you are suffering because of sin. Otherwise, remember—we must go through many hardships to enter the kingdom of God.

∾

"You will have suffering in this world. Be courageous! I have conquered the world."
    —John 16:33

When they had appointed elders in every
church . . . they committed them to the Lord
in whom they had believed.
  —Acts 14:23

∽

Paul and Barnabas wanted to leave
the new believers with ongoing strength
and encouragement, so they carefully
appointed elders in the church who were
not only spiritually mature but also (if
I may say so gently)—*old!*

However, older men were not the only
ones charged with responsibility. In the
book of Titus, we learn that Paul also
charged older women, younger women,
and younger men to faithful service.
It sounds to me like He chooses to use
people of every age whose hearts are
turned to Him.

Life is difficult. The converts in Lystra, Iconium, and Pisidian Antioch were surely strengthened and encouraged as they saw living examples of people who were surviving hardships with victory and joy. Listening to Paul and Barnabas testify must have greatly impacted their ability to endure.

We don't have Paul and Barnabas, but we have hosts of older people who are more than happy to tell us about the faithfulness of God—if we'll just stop, ask them, and listen.

∾

Even when I am old and gray, God, do not abandon me. Then I will proclaim Your power to another generation, Your strength to all who are to come.
   —Psalm 71:18

"Why, then, are you now testing God by putting on the disciples' necks a yoke that neither our forefathers nor we have been able to bear?"
—Acts 15:10

∽

Like a leech, legalism saps the lifeblood out of its victim. It enters the door in the name of righteousness to vacuum out all the dirt and then ends up vacuuming out all the spirit.

Do you have impossible expectations of other people? Do you expect things from them you wouldn't want to have to deliver yourself? Do you expect near perfection in your children and tireless commitment from your coworkers? Are you a yoke breaker just looking for an unsuspecting neck?

Yoke breakers are miserable people because they are never satisfied with less than perfection. Their obsession with everyone else's lack of perfection helps them keep their minds off their own.

Let's return to the simplicity of salvation. Not adding to. Not taking away. When we paint the picture of our salvation for others to see, we may use different colors, textures, and shapes on the edges of the parchment. But in the center can only be a cross. Anything else cheapens grace and cheats the believer. Paul wasn't about to let that happen to his beloved flock.

❧

Christ has liberated us into freedom. Therefore stand firm and don't submit again to a yoke of slavery.
    —Galatians 5:1

*For it was the Holy Spirit's decision—
and ours—to put no greater burden on
you than these necessary things.*
    —Acts 15:28

∽

The believers in Antioch were told to
abstain from food sacrificed to idols.
Gentile believers might have reasoned
that although they would not dream of
sacrificing to idols anymore, what harm
could be done by simply buying the
leftover food at a good price after it was
offered? Were they free from the Jewish
law or not?

Satan sometimes tempts us the same way.
We don't desire to go back to our old
lifestyles, but certain parts of it seem so
harmless—some of the old friends, the
old hangouts, and the old refreshments.

The elders wisely warned them that nothing is harmless about the practices of the old life. Eating food sacrificed to idols could weaken them to former practices or cause someone else to stumble. The Gentile believers would not forfeit their gift of grace by doing so, but they would risk their freedom and also compromise their separateness.

They were wise to avoid anything that would place them close enough to the vacuum to be sucked back in. Safety and freedom are found in staying so far away that you can't even hear the vacuum cleaner running.

∽

As obedient children, do not be conformed to the desires of your former ignorance.
    —1 Peter 1:14

Barnabas wanted to take along John Mark.
But Paul did not think it appropriate to take
along this man who had deserted them.
   —Acts 15:37–38

∽

Paul and Barnabas both were Spirit-filled
servants of God, yet they differed on
whether John Mark should join them.
We might assume that either Paul or
Barnabas was not under the leadership of
the Holy Spirit; after all, the Spirit could
not possess two opinions. Or could He?

I believe both men could have been
under the direct influence of the Holy
Spirit and yet still have differed. How?
The Spirit might have been saying yes to
Barnabas and no to Paul. He might have
wanted Barnabas, not Paul, to take John
Mark so God could divide and multiply.

As a result of differing convictions, two preachers became four. Paul and Barnabas went their separate ways—two mentors, each with a new apprentice. Can you imagine how much simpler church life could be if we accepted that God could place two people under different convictions to multiply ministry?

Often differences erupt due to two opinionated people unwilling to budge. On the other hand, when God leads two people who have walked together to a fork in the road, He can do something wonderful—if they and their constituents are mature enough to deal with it!

∽

Accept anyone who is weak in faith, but don't argue about doubtful issues.
   —Romans 14:1

There was such a sharp disagreement that
they parted company, and Barnabas took
Mark with him and sailed off to Cyprus.
  —Acts 15:39

∽

We may sometimes find ourselves
strongly differing with someone about
matters related to church or ministry.
But differing convictions don't have to
become razor-sharp contentions.

First, identify the real source of the
argument. Part of spiritual maturity is
risking our position in favor of the will
and glory of God.

Second, submit the issue to God. When
we remove all selfish, worldly motives
and influences, the issues often either
disappear or shrink to a workable level.

Third, resist the temptation to sin in your anger. Each of us regrets something we've said or done in anger. When we are mad at another believer, let's ask God's help so our feelings don't turn into wrong action.

Finally, pray for (and if at all possible, *with*) the other person involved. Prayer changes things and people! Can you imagine how defeated the enemy would become if two divided church leaders or laymen got down on their knees together and prayed for God's glory? We don't have to be together on every issue, but we can be together in prayer!

✆

Arrogance leads to nothing but strife, but wisdom is gained by those who take advice.
—Proverbs 13:10

I long to see you so that I may be filled with joy, clearly recalling your sincere faith that first lived in your grandmother Lois, then in your mother Eunice.

—2 Timothy 1:4–5

෨

We've almost become convinced that bad influences are stronger than good. Paul's young protégé Timothy certainly is evidence to the contrary. We have a wonderful biblical precedent proving that godly influence can carry a much heavier weight than ungodly influence.

Lois and Eunice lived out their faith. Timothy saw in them genuine examples of faithfulness. Their lives were devoted to God even when the company left. They were genuine—not perfect, but real. And their sincerity won Timothy to the truth.

When a parent practices sin and rebellion against God, adversely affected children and grandchildren can share some of the same tendencies. But sin and rebellion are not the only heritage passed down to future generations. Faithfulness has an even greater influence.

Yes, you can rear godly children in spite of imperfect circumstances. So hang in there, parent! Let your children see the sincerity of your faith. Let them see you praying and trusting. Nothing carries the weight of sincere faith!

∽

"Only be on your guard and diligently watch yourselves, so that you don't forget the things your eyes have seen and so that they don't slip from your mind as long as you live."
  —Deuteronomy 4:9

Above all, put on love—the perfect bond of
unity. And let the peace of the Messiah, to
which you were also called in one body,
control your hearts.
    —Colossians 3:14–15

~

Peace is one of the most obvious ear-
marks of the authority of Christ. A sense
of peace will virtually always accompany
His will and direction—even when the
direction might not be our personal
preference. On the other hand, a lack of
peace will often accompany a mistaken
path—even when the direction is
definitely our personal preference.

Remember, Christ is the Prince of Peace.
His peace will accompany His authority.
Learn to recognize peace as one of God's
prompters.

Paul and his fellow servants were pliable when God prompted them not to enter the province of Asia by removing their sense of peace and approval. They were willing for God to change their plans.

More than any other disciple, Paul was used of God to teach about the activity of the Holy Spirit. But Paul could not teach what he had never learned. He learned to follow the leadership of the Holy Spirit one day at a time, one city at a time. Let's learn from his example and be willing to change our course when we sense God has different plans.

∽

The peace of God, which surpasses every thought, will guard your hearts and your minds in Christ Jesus.
    —Philippians 4:7

A woman named Lydia, a dealer in purple
cloth from the city of Thyatira, who worshiped
God, was listening. The Lord opened her heart
to pay attention to what was spoken by Paul.
   —Acts 16:14

∽

We've seen Paul have more thrilling
encounters than this one with Lydia.
Nothing outwardly dramatic happened.
Almost seemed ho-hum, didn't it? Was
this all that God had in mind—one
woman's reception of the gospel?

But after temporarily closing a door in
the province of Asia, God strained their
eyes to see a much wider vision. The
gospel of Jesus Christ went to Europe!
Within a couple hundred years after this
single event, Christians numbered in the
tens of thousands there.

And it all started with a businesswoman named Lydia.

For anyone who ever wondered if God could use a professional businesswoman, meet Lydia. She was a city girl, a salesperson. A homeowner with enough room for a host of people. Yet her professional life was balanced by the priorities of her spiritual life. She made herself available to God. Because she did, "the Lord opened her heart" to hear Paul's message. And God gave birth to the gospel in Europe. I'd say this businesswoman had a pretty important ministry, wouldn't you?

∾

You will know that the Lord of Hosts has sent me to you. For who scorns the day of small things?
   —*Zechariah 4:9–10*

"These men are seriously disturbing our city. They are Jews, and are promoting customs that are not legal for us as Romans to adopt or practice."
—Acts 16:20–21

⌇

Four men preached the gospel in Philippi, but only two of them were punished. Where were Luke and Timothy when the sparks started flying?

The Roman world had recently experienced a fresh surge of anti-Semitism, and Emperor Claudius had expelled all Jews from Rome. Timothy and Luke may have been considered Gentiles by the Roman authorities. Paul and Silas, on the other hand, were dragged before a strongly anti-Semitic magistrate and persecuted because of their Jewish heritage.

Imagine how the foursome felt: divided over their backgrounds, two were freed, and two were carried away maliciously. I'm not at all sure which two had the easier sentence.

God is very aware that standing close to someone who is hurting hurts! He does it every day. But whether we are the ones suffering or we're alongside another, His grace is sufficient for our need. So you can cry out for help, even when you're hurting for someone else. He'll hear you and acknowledge your need!

∾

In all their suffering, He suffered,
and the Angel of His Presence saved them.
He redeemed them because of His love
and compassion.
    —Isaiah 63:9

*About midnight Paul and Silas were praying
and singing hymns to God, and the prisoners
were listening to them.*
  —Acts 16:25

∾

These two bloodied servants of God—
Paul and Silas—had been taken to a
dungeon and placed in stocks, unable to
move, pain wracking their bodies. Yet
though they were bound in iron chains,
they found the freedom to sing.

Prayers come naturally when we are
distressed—but songs? Finding notes is
difficult when your body is gripped with
pain. Nonetheless, these few notes found
their way into a melody; their melodies
turned into hymns. Every stanza issued
a fresh strength and their voices were
unchained, penetrating walls and bars.

When praise is the last thing that comes naturally to us and we choose to worship Him anyway, we've had the privilege of offering a genuine sacrifice of praise.

When we sing a midnight song or speak praises in the darkest hours, the chains of hopelessness not only drop from our ankles but sometimes from the ankles of those who listen. We can preach the gospel in many ways, but the message is never more clear than when God's people refuse to cease their praises during intense suffering.

∾

The LORD will send His faithful love by day;
His song will be with me in the night—
a prayer to the God of my life.
    —Psalm 42:8

As usual, Paul went to them, and on three Sabbath days reasoned with them from the Scriptures.
—Acts 17:2

∽

Paul and Silas had traveled a hundred miles from Philippi to Thessalonica without the benefit of a motorized vehicle. They seemed to know exactly where they wanted to go and certainly did not lack the stamina to get there!

What criteria made one city more of a priority than another? Obviously the first criteria was the leadership of the Holy Spirit. Paul cited another criteria in Romans 15:20, when he declared, "My aim is to evangelize where Christ has not been named, in order that I will not be building on someone else's foundation."

God used both of these principles: the leadership of the Holy Spirit and Paul's desire to go into territories untouched by the gospel. And in each new venue, not only did Paul customarily preach in the synagogues first, he employed the same method each time. He sought to prove that Jesus was the Christ with the Old Testament Scripture.

I believe the reason Paul used this method with them was because God had used it so effectively on him in the desert of Arabia. He knew this technique could work on the hardest of hearts because it had worked so well on his.

∽

All Scripture is inspired by God and is profitable for teaching.
  —2 Timothy 3:16

*They welcomed the message with eagerness
and examined the Scriptures daily to see if
these things were so.*
  —Acts 17:11

∽

All believers have the right to ask
questions and examine the Scriptures to
check the accuracy of the teaching they
hear. Congregations can be easily misled
if they do not feel or exercise the freedom
to double-check teaching and preaching
against the Word of God.

A savvy communicator can use the
Scriptures taken out of context to teach
almost anything! Any portion of Scripture must be compared with Scripture as
a whole. The enemy of our souls will use
every means and every human agent he
can to topple us. And if all we have going

for us are the opinions of men through sermons or lessons, little will be left when life shakes us up. But when we've learned to examine the Scriptures for ourselves, we have a few things nailed down when life starts to rock.

As you continue to study the Word of God, one nailed-down, personally discovered truth will turn into many, and you will be better equipped to face anything that comes your way. Nothing will profit you more than learning to examine the Scriptures for yourself.

∽

The revelation of Your words brings light and gives understanding to the inexperienced. I pant with open mouth because I long for Your commands.
    —Psalm 119:130–131

While Paul was waiting for them in Athens,
his spirit was troubled within him when he
saw that the city was full of idols.
    —Acts 17:16

∽

Paul had to encounter the imposing city
of Athens all by himself. And according
to Acts 17:16, he reacted strongly to the
sight of a city full of idols. Imagine going
on a mission trip to a city like Varanasi,
India—a Hindu holy city filled with
temples and images depicting hundreds
of gods.

Yet here we have a tender opportunity to
see the sincerity of Paul's heart, for "he
reasoned in the synagogue with the Jews
and with those who worshiped God, and
in the marketplace every day with those
who happened to be there" (v. 17).

He had no emotional or spiritual support
and probably little physical support.
None of the others would have known if
he had simply been too intimidated to
preach. No one would have blamed him
anyway. Yet day by day he tried to reason
with any Athenian who would listen,
because he was so concerned that they
needed Jesus Christ.

What keeps you the most distracted
and unaware of openings for spiritual
conversation with others? What could
make you more tuned in and prepared for
these sharing opportunities?

༄

Your speech should always be gracious,
seasoned with salt, so that you may know
how you should answer each person.
    —Colossians 4:6

Some began to ridicule him. But others said,
"We will hear you about this again." So Paul
went out from their presence.
  —Acts 17:32–33

∽

Paul was not persecuted in Athens, nor
was he forced to leave the city. He simply
left. A few sneered; others were polite
enough to say they would be willing to
listen to his strange teachings again. But
most never realized Paul was escorted
into town by the one true God. And
most never cared.

Acts 17 has changed the way I pray
about the nations. I cannot count the
times I've asked God to crumble the spirit
of opposition and persecution in many
nations where Christians are a small
fighting force.

I will still continue to ask God to strengthen and protect those facing opposition and persecution. However, I now find my heart drawn across the map to places where a quieter dragon of perhaps equal force has made its den— the spirit of indifference.

Christianity can grow and flourish under some of the most difficult opposition, but it will prosper very little where people refuse to be changed by it. Paul's experience in Athens proves that the best of sermons will never change an unwilling person's heart.

∽

You have commanded that Your precepts be diligently kept. If only my ways were committed to keeping Your statutes!
—Psalm 119:4–5

When I came to you, brothers, announcing the testimony of God to you, I did not come with brilliance of speech or wisdom.
  —*1 Corinthians 2:1*

∽

On the miles between Athens and Corinth, Paul probably hashed and rehashed his experiences. He wished he had said this or that. During those long hours, I believe he convinced himself that every effort in Athens had failed. I suspect he became so focused on the negative that he lost sight of the positive.

Paul had been the pride of his graduating class—the child prodigy! So imagine the beating his ego took in Athens. By the time he reached Corinth, he had "determined to know nothing . . . except Jesus Christ and Him crucified" (1 Cor. 2:2).

Thank goodness, he knew the only thing he really had to know! He determined to base his life and ministry on Christ—his one certainty!

The enemy would have enjoyed preventing Paul from ministering in Corinth because of feelings of inadequacy, but Satan was unsuccessful. God instead used Paul's feelings to give a great "demonstration of the Spirit and power" (1 Cor. 2:4).

God sometimes uses us most powerfully when we feel the least adequate.

∽

"I will give you such words and a wisdom that none of your adversaries will be able to resist or contradict."
     —Luke 21:15

God has chosen the world's foolish things
to shame the wise, and God has chosen the
world's weak things to shame the strong.
   —1 Corinthians 1:27

∽

Paul explained why God often proves Himself when we feel we have the least to offer: so we can be clear that the power comes from Him and not from us. Paul concluded, "The one who boasts must boast in the Lord" (1 Cor. 1:31).

Just before the taping of my first video series, God allowed me to go through a very difficult time. My confidence took a severe beating. I was so emotionally exhausted that I did not know how I would get through the taping. I walked out on that set with only enough strength to get on my knees and pray.

But when I got up off my knees to teach, a stream of strength seemed to pour from heaven. Never in my adult life have I had less confidence, yet He gave me enough of His to keep my knees from buckling.

Perhaps God has opened a door for you, but you have no confidence. Is insecurity holding you back from the ministry God has for you? Each of us struggles with insecurities and the loss of confidence. No one has ever been used more mightily than the apostle Paul, yet he was so scared at times he made himself sick!

&

Therefore, I will most gladly boast all the more about my weaknesses, so that Christ's power may reside in me.
   —2 Corinthians 12:9

Paul, having stayed on for many days, said good-bye to the brothers and sailed away to Syria. . . . He shaved his head at Cenchreae, because he had taken a vow.

—Acts 18:18

∽

Why in the world would we need to know Paul got a haircut? Actually, this verse holds a primary key to understanding Paul's visit to Corinth.

Paul's haircut resulted from a vow he had made, most likely the Nazarite vow. Remember, Paul was a Jewish Christian. His Jewish heritage was deeply rooted. He understood that Christ did not save him to make him forget his heritage but to complete it. At times he still applied some of the former practices of the Jew, not as legalities but as wise choices.

If an Israelite was going through a time when he or she felt the necessity to be extraordinarily consecrated to God—usually a time of extremely difficult circumstances or temptation—the person would voluntarily take this vow. They knew that in order to be victorious or obedient, they needed extra help and concentration on God.

Paul's actions teach us an important lesson. We obviously need to avoid temptation, but when we can't help but face it, we can prepare ourselves.

∾

I discipline my body and bring it under strict control, so that after preaching to others, I myself will not be disqualified.
   —*1 Corinthians 9:27*

*He left them there, but he himself entered the
synagogue and engaged in discussion with the
Jews. And though they asked him to stay for a
longer time, he declined.*
   —Acts 18:19–20

∽

Paul so desperately wanted his fellow
Jews to know Christ that, if possible, he
would have died for them. He had not
finished preaching to the Jews altogether.
So in Ephesus he went right back to the
synagogue and reasoned with them again.
He must have been ecstatic over the
favorable response of the Jews there.

But again we see why Paul was such an
effective minister and servant. He had
surrendered his life to the leadership of
the Holy Spirit. He was not driven by his
own desires and rationalizations.

In his position, I might have convinced myself I was supposed to remain in Ephesus, at least for a while, based on my own desires to see God do a work among a people I loved and an apparent open door. They were begging for more! Yet Acts 18:20 tells us he declined. Paul firmly and lovingly said no.

Paul's example teaches us a timely lesson. The fact that a need exists does not mean God has called me to meet that need. We are wise to trust Him when He seems to be leading us contrary to those things we want to do or those things that seem to be so rational and fitting.

∽

Seek the Lord, *all you humble of the earth, who carry out what He commands.*
    —*Zephaniah 2:3*

*Since there is envy and strife among
you, are you not fleshly and living like
ordinary people?*
  —1 Corinthians 3:3

∽

We get a good glimpse into human
nature as Paul addresses the believers in
Corinth. They had responded to those
who came and preached to them by
forming warring camps. The people had
reacted much like we react today. We
tend to compare Christian leaders and
fall into camps behind our choices.

We must make a concerted effort to avoid
this. Each of us could cite an example,
but every branch of in-depth Bible study
has loyal supporters who swear by that
particular method or teacher. Some
would rather fight than switch.

God is joyfully using many different methods and styles to accomplish His goal of equipping His church to be effective and holy during difficult days. He has raised many fine teachers and preachers for this time. Let's reap the benefit of as many as possible and value their contributions whether they are magnetic like Apollos, analytical like Luke, forthright like Paul, or warm like Priscilla and Aquila.

Paul didn't mince words. His answer to those who were camping around certain speakers? Oh, grow up!

∽

I want you to know, brothers, that the gospel preached by me is not based on a human point of view.
    —Galatians 1:11

[Paul] asked them, "Did you receive the Holy Spirit when you believed?" "No," they told him, "we haven't even heard that there is a Holy Spirit."
—Acts 19:2

∽

These original converts knew virtually nothing about the Holy Spirit. Even their knowledge of the Old Testament didn't help much because the Spirit's activity on earth was so different after the coming of Christ than it had been before.

God knew the concept of the Holy Spirit would be difficult for new believers to understand as He raised up His church, so God made His Spirit obvious. He sometimes accompanied His Spirit with a sudden physical evidence such as speaking in tongues.

Few topics have caused division like speaking in tongues. But no matter what you believe about this issue, Paul was clear on at least two points concerning the activity of the Holy Spirit: 1) All believers are baptized by the Holy Spirit. The Spirit resides in all believers equally. 2) Not all believers spoke in tongues.

Many believe God never uses the gift of tongues today. Many others believe God always gives the gift of tongues to every true believer. I think we are wise to avoid words like *always* and *never*. He told us to love one another, not judge one another.

∽

I want their hearts to be encouraged and joined together in love, so that they may have all the riches of assured understanding.
    —Colossians 2:2

*When some became hardened and would not
believe, slandering the Way in front of the
crowd, he withdrew from them and met
separately with the disciples.*

 —Acts 19:9

∽

God performs His work in countless
ways we cannot see. He remains active in
our lives even when we are unaware,
even when we feel defeated, unwelcome,
and misunderstood.

Take, for example, the bountiful fruit
produced from Paul's Bible study, begun
in the midst of rejection. Within two
years, according to Acts 19:10, "all the
inhabitants of the province of Asia, both
Jews and Greeks, heard the word of the
Lord." The churches of Laodicea, Colosse,
and Hierapolis were founded as a result.

Like Gideon's army, a few well-trained soldiers in the Lord's service can be more effective than hundreds who have never been discipled. God honors His Word and often overtly blesses discipleship with fruit far beyond human effort.

Paul was an effective teacher, but God still produced fruit in greater measure than his labor. When a few seeds produce a huge crop, God is up to something supernatural! Acknowledge it and praise Him! He makes obvious His blessing on true discipleship.

∾

Be on your guard, so that you are not led away by the error of the immoral and fall from your own stability. But grow in the grace and knowledge of our Lord and Savior Jesus Christ.
    —2 Peter 3:17–18

*God was performing extraordinary miracles
by Paul's hands.*
    —Acts 19:11

∽

Sometimes I am completely perplexed by
God's willingness to humor us. When He
wanted to lead the Magi to the Christ
child, He did not use a mark in the sand.
He led them through a star because they
were stargazers—then He went beyond
anything they had ever seen.

In the same way, when God wanted to
lead the Ephesians to the Savior, He got
their attention through supernatural
phenomena because that's where *they*
were looking. God wants to be found.
He is so gracious to show up right where
we are looking—so He can take us
beyond anything we've ever seen.

God sometimes reveals Himself to a homeless man hiding under a bridge through a blanket brought to him by a caring minister. He sometimes reveals Himself to a drunk through a servant who cares for him and offers him Living Water. He sometimes reveals Himself to a prostitute through a godly police officer who tells her Christ can set her free.

God doesn't wait for people to come to Him. He intervenes right at the point of their need. He's looking for a few brave people, like the apostle Paul, who are willing to go rather than wait for them to come. May we be some of those people.

∽

We were pleased to share with you not only the gospel of God but also our own lives.
—*1 Thessalonians 2:8*

Though Paul wanted to go in before the people, the disciples did not let him.
  —Acts 19:30

∽

Based on Paul's willingness to address the hostile crowd in Ephesus, we may assume that he sometimes had more courage than sense! He was going to speak out on behalf of Christianity no matter what!

Also based on verse 30, I believe Paul's disciples were not afraid to disagree with him. He was not a religious dictator who surrounded himself with yes-men.

I am impressed by a third assumption as well: Paul sometimes let the wisdom of others take precedence over his own desires. I am refreshed by leaders who do not think they always have to be right.

One more assumption I would like to make is based on verse 31, which talks about his "friends" among the provincial officials. Paul obviously had many good friends from every walk of life.

We tend to describe people in phrases: he's funny; she's always so bossy; he's such a controlling person; she never fails to be upbeat. But God created humans as the most complex creatures alive. None of us can be wrapped up in a single phrase. Yes, Paul could be unyielding, but he could also be persuaded. He could be tough, and he could be gracious. He was perhaps not so different from the rest of us!

∽

God has placed the parts, each one of them, in the body just as He wanted.
    —1 Corinthians 12:18

When they recognized that he was a Jew, a united cry went up from all of them for about two hours: "Great is Artemis of the Ephesians!"
   —Acts 19:34

∾

The Ephesians believed the image of Artemis had fallen from heaven. Some scholars assume they were describing a meteor that had hit Ephesus, one that the people had thought to look like a multi-breasted woman. Therefore, they assumed it was the goddess Artemis and hailed her as the deity of childbirth.

I am sometimes amazed at the things people believe. A number of years ago, I prepared to teach the book of Genesis in Sunday school. In an attempt to be prepared for questions and rebuttals, I studied the theory of evolution.

At times I laughed out loud. I couldn't believe that this theory is taught as fact in many public schools. After a fairly in-depth comparison, I decided it took far more faith to believe in evolution than creation!

When Paul came to Ephesus, he brought the message of a Messiah sent from God who offers eternal life to every individual who believes. I'm no rocket scientist, but I find Paul's message far more believable than a goddess falling out of heaven in the form of a meteor. Go ahead and believe Him. He's very believable.

∽

You love Him, though you have not seen Him. And though not seeing Him now, you believe in Him.
    —*1 Peter 1:8*

A young man named Eutychus was sitting on a window sill and sank into a deep sleep as Paul kept on speaking.

—Acts 20:9

∾

Picture this scene with me a moment. A large group of people were gathered in one room, and the lamps provided just enough heat to make the atmosphere cozy and warm. Most of the listeners had awakened with the rising sun, and the time was now approaching midnight. Eutychus was sitting in the windowsill, trying to stay attentive.

The young man's eyelids would drop; then he would force them open. He finally fell into a deep sleep, probably had a dream that caused him to jump, and out the window he flew.

This story would not be humorous without the happy ending. God raised Eutychus from the dead! What a relief! A wonderfully rare phenomenon took place that day.

I find myself amused once again as the scene ends. Paul went back to business as usual. He climbed three flights of stairs, broke bread with them, and talked until daylight. All in a day's work. I have a feeling no one fell asleep this time!

My moral to the story: may God bring back to life whom man hath put to sleep.

∽

Your dead will live; their bodies will rise.
Awake and sing, you who dwell in the dust!
  —Isaiah 26:19

"You know, from the first day I set foot in Asia, how I was with you the whole time."
   —Acts 20:18

∽

Like a father with only a few moments left to share his heart with his children, Paul shared things with the Ephesians that were priority to him. He reminded them of the attention he had given to their needs. He shared his assumptions, his ambition, his heartfelt admonition, and his deep affection.

I believe Paul was so attentive to them because he became involved emotionally as well as spiritually. I believe he poured himself out among them as much or more than any other group to whom he ministered. They not only saw his humility; they saw his heart.

He did not hide from them his tears or the pain of his hardships. He was open with them about his past sin and his feelings of unworthiness in the ministry God had given him. The Ephesians knew Paul was genuine. He approached them withholding nothing. He did not hesitate to preach anything that would be helpful.

He loved them enough to teach them anything and everything that would be of benefit, even if they didn't like it. He was willing to hurt their feelings momentarily if it would help their hearts eternally.

∽

It is right for me to think this way about all of you, because I have you in my heart, and you are all partners with me in grace.
    —Philippians 1:7

In town after town the Holy Spirit testifies
to me that chains and afflictions are waiting
for me.
    —Acts 20:23

∽

Paul was so determined to be faithful
to the task God had assigned him, even
the certainty of his suffering could not
dissuade him.

Fear is a very powerful tool. Don't think
for a moment Satan did not try to use fear
to hinder the apostle from fulfilling God's
purposes, and don't think Paul was not
terrified at times. Of course he was. To
think otherwise would be to minimize
his faithfulness. Paul was afraid, but his
love for Christ exceeded his fear of
suffering and death. His main ambition
was to finish his task faithfully.

Notice the phrase in verse 24: "the ministry I received from the Lord Jesus." Paul felt no responsibility to complete the task Christ had given to Peter or Barnabas or Timothy. He believed and taught that God has specific plans for each believer.

God has a task for you—one He planned very long ago and suited for our present generation. Remember you are not responsible for completing anyone else's task, just yours. God wants us to encourage one another in our tasks, but we are responsible only for completing our own.

∽

It is not the one commending himself who is approved, but the one the Lord commends.
—*2 Corinthians 10:18*

Be on guard for yourselves and for all the flock,
among whom the Holy Spirit has appointed
you as overseers.
    —Acts 20:28

～

Paul named two groups the elders were
to keep watch over: themselves and the
flock God had given them. What an
important message to us! We can hardly
keep watch over a group if we don't keep
watch over ourselves!

Many leaders have seasons when their
lives seem temporarily out of control.
Most people who have served God for
decades have had a season in which they
got off course. Those who never depart
from the course in many years of service
deserve our highest commendations,
but they are rare.

I do not believe a leader who temporarily veers off-track should be disqualified from ever leading again. Yet we are wise leaders to step out of leadership when we are having a difficult time staying on the course. We cannot lead others to a place to which we are not steering our own lives as well.

We don't have to be church elders for these words and warnings to apply to us. If God has assigned you a flock, you have a serious responsibility to keep a close watch over your own life and also to care deeply for theirs.

∽

Shepherd God's flock among you, not overseeing out of compulsion but freely, according to God's will.
    —1 Peter 5:2

All of them, with their wives and children, escorted us out of the city. After kneeling down on the beach to pray, we said good-bye to one another.

—Acts 21:5–6

ᔍ

Have you noticed how often God brings blessings to the unscheduled stops along our way? God had a blessing waiting for Paul and the others on their unscheduled stop while in the city of Tyre.

Christians had been planted in Phoenicia, the region in which Tyre was located, having been scattered by the same wave of persecution in which Stephen was martyred. Don't forget how deeply Paul, then known as Saul, had been involved in the persecution that caused these believers to flee for their lives.

Yet I never cease to be amazed at the hospitality of believers in the New Testament church. Their hearts were so instantly bound with his, they begged him not to go to Jerusalem.

Just picture what the sand must have looked like after Paul boarded the ship and the crowd went back home. Footprints leading to and from the shore. Then nothing but knee prints clustered together in the damp sand. A sight for God to behold. Long after the tide washed away every print, the power of those prayers was still at work.

ဢ

Don't neglect to show hospitality, for by doing this some have welcomed angels as guests without knowing it.
  —Hebrews 13:2

Paul replied, "What are you doing, weeping and breaking my heart?"
—Acts 21:13

∽

Though Paul could hardly tear himself away from the Ephesian elders in Acts 20 who feared for his safety in Jerusalem, he never wavered in his resolve. He also remained unmoved when the disciples in Tyre urged him to stay. Yet we see him respond with enormous emotion when his beloved associates—Luke, Timothy, and the others—wept and pleaded with him not to go.

We sometimes feel as if we're playing tug-of-war with God. In bitter tears we let go of the rope, tumble to the ground, and cry, "Have your way, God! You're going to do what You want anyway!"

God is not playing a game. He doesn't jerk on the rope just so He can win. In fact, He doesn't want us to let go of the rope at all. Rather than see us drop the rope and give up, He wants us to hang on and let Him pull us over to His side.

God's will is always best even when we cannot imagine how. Surrendering to His will doesn't mean you lose. Ultimately it means you win. Keep hanging on to that rope and let Him pull you over to His side. One day you'll understand. And you'll see His glory.

∽

Since he would not be persuaded, we stopped talking and simply said, "The Lord's will be done!"
    —Acts 21:14

*"They have been told about you that you teach
all the Jews who are among the Gentiles to
abandon Moses."*
    —Acts 21:21

৶

Paul expected to face opposition from
unbelievers in Jerusalem, but to be hit
immediately by the disapproval of fellow
believers must have drained his energy
and excitement. Much of what they were
saying about him wasn't even accurate.

Perhaps you know how Paul felt when
he met disapproval among his own and
found he had been misunderstood. Have
you ever thought, "I expected this kind
of thing from unbelievers, but I wasn't
expecting this from my own fellow
believers"? If so, you are part of a large
fraternity, with Paul as a charter member.

Several times in Paul's ministry he was placed in a similar position with both Jews and Gentiles. He said that though he was free in Christ, he made himself a slave to everyone so that he could win as many as possible. He said he became like a Jew to the Jews in order to win the Jews, and like a Gentile to the Gentiles in order to win the Gentiles.

Like Paul, each of us must seek common ground with those who do not know Christ. We can respond legalistically and shun harmless practices, but if we do, we risk alienating the very people we want to reach.

∽

I have become all things to all people,
so that I may by all means save some.
  —1 Corinthians 9:22

*When Paul got to the steps, he had to be
carried by the soldiers because of the mob's
violence, for the mass of people were following
and yelling, "Kill him!"*
  —Acts 21:35–36

〜

Paul had expected to be seized, but I'm
not sure expectation and preparation are
always synonymous. Was he ready for
hatred and wholesale rejection by the
people he would have given his life for?
I'm not sure how adequately a person can
prepare for such pain.

Paul had received Christ by faith, knew
Christ by name, but came face-to-face
with Christ through experience. On this
particular day in Jerusalem, Paul experienced a fellowship in His sufferings
unlike any he had ever encountered.

Both Christ and Paul knew suffering was inevitable. Both knew they would end up giving their lives—One as the Savior of the world, the other as His servant. Both of them grieved over Jerusalem. Both felt compelled to return to the holy city. Both knew the horror of being swept up in an angry mob, experiencing the newness of every rejection. But one can hardly prepare for people who wish you dead.

Paul did not know what would happen to him, but he did know Christ. And as the apostle fellowshipped in His sufferings, he had never known Jesus better.

~

My goal is to know Him and the power of His resurrection and the fellowship of His sufferings, being conformed to His death.
   —Philippians 3:10

"Brothers and fathers, listen now to my defense before you."
—Acts 22:1

༄

Few of us have experienced the dramatic conversion Paul went on to describe in Acts 22, but don't think your testimony is meaningless on that basis. Every conversion cost the same amount of Christ's blood shed on the cross. Yours is just as meaningful as the most dramatic conversion ever told.

In the parable of the prodigal son, the elder brother felt insulted because the father accepted his brother after a season of wild living. He didn't understand the biggest difference between the two brothers was that the prodigal son had to live with the personal loss and suffering.

If your conversion was less sensational than others, praise God for less drama! With it probably came less pain! You don't have to see a bright light from heaven to have a story to tell others. The determining factor is not how exciting your conversion was but how excited you are now about your conversion.

As we share our testimonies, we can help unbelievers see all that we've gained since Jesus came into our hearts, all the ways our lives have been blessed and enhanced by His presence within us. We often have no idea how much people are struggling to find a reason to live.

∽

I live by faith in the Son of God, who loved me and gave Himself for me.
   —*Galatians* 2:20

They listened to him up to this word. Then they raised their voices, shouting, "Wipe this person off the earth—it's a disgrace for him to live!"

—Acts 22:22

∽

On a human scale we cannot judge Paul's visit to Jerusalem a success. Perhaps his experiences in places like this will teach us to think differently about success and failure. Hopefully we will come to understand that in our Christian lives, success is obedience to God, not results we can measure.

Was he a failure because they rejected him? Was his testimony shared in vain? Absolutely not. God had given Paul an opportunity to share his testimony with the people who had just tried to kill him.

Did they hear Paul's message? Oh, yes. Otherwise, they wouldn't have responded so emotionally. Few of those in hearing distance that day forgot Paul's testimony. We cannot judge effectiveness from immediate results. When we obey God, we find great comfort in leaving the consequences up to Him.

Paul received little encouragement to preach while he was there—yet he continued. Paul's certainty of what he had been called to do was exceeded only by his certainty of who called. Paul considered Him who called worth it all.

∾

The God of all grace, who called you to His eternal glory in Christ Jesus, will personally restore, establish, strengthen, and support you.
—1 Peter 5:10

*Paul looked intently at the Sanhedrin and
said, "Brothers, I have lived my life before God
in all good conscience until this day."*
—Acts 23:1

∾

By itself, all the conscience can do with
a guilty person is condemn. But the Holy
Spirit who resides in us supplies abun-
dant power not only to recognize the
right thing, but to do it!

Can we really have clear consciences?
Considering Paul's past, if he can have a
clear conscience, any of us can. Like me,
you may have discovered that asking God
for forgiveness doesn't always make you
feel better. Sometimes we know we're
forgiven, but we still feel a load of guilt.
How can we discover the freedom of a
clear conscience?

Picture the cross of Christ. Really take a good mental look at it. Was Christ's death on the cross enough to cover your sin? Enough to take away your guilt? Yes. He gave everything He had for everything we've said, done, or thought.

Then picture yourself at the foot of His cross, close enough to have your heart cleansed by His redemptive blood. No sin is too grievous. No load is too heavy for Christ to carry. Walk away free, and leave behind with God that old condemning tape you've been playing over and over on your mental recorder!

∽

Let us draw near with a true heart in full assurance of faith, our hearts sprinkled clean from an evil conscience.
    —Hebrews 10:22

*The high priest Ananias ordered those who
were standing next to him to strike him on the
mouth. Then Paul said to him, "God is going
to strike you, you whitewashed wall!"*
    —Acts 23:2–3

∽

Unfortunately we don't have the benefit
of hearing Paul's voice inflection in this
verse. But his response toward Ananias
suggests he might have been ready for an
altercation. I believe he knew he was
insulting the high priest and probably
offended him further by saying, in effect,
"Sorry, but I never would have recognized this guy as a high priest."

No doubt Paul knew he was insulting the
high priest. He was far too knowledge-
able not to have recognized Ananias's
robes and obvious position of honor.

I'm suggesting Paul may have been (if I may be so bold) in a touch of an insolent mood. I mean absolutely no disrespect, but I believe he sometimes struggled with a temper. And when dealing with a foe like Ananias, whom history recalls as an insolent, hot-tempered man, the sight of his false piety and that of the other religious leaders probably made Paul's stomach turn—especially because he had been one of them.

Sometimes the ugliest picture we see of ourselves is the one we see in others. And even a great man like Paul can find it to be more than he can take.

∽

Evildoers will be destroyed, but those who put their hope in the Lord *will inherit the land.*
   —Psalm 37:9

The Lord stood by him and said, "Have
courage! For as you have testified about Me in
Jerusalem, so you must also testify in Rome."
—Acts 23:11

❧

Why did Christ draw so physically
close to Paul at this moment? I believe
Paul was overcome with fear and may
have been convinced he would not live
much longer. He had looked straight into
the eyes of rage. He was separated from
his friends. He was imprisoned by
strangers. I believe he was terrified.

Later Paul wrote from another prison
cell, "My God will supply all your needs
according to His riches in glory in Christ
Jesus" (Phil. 4:19). He could make such a
claim because God had been so faithful to
meet his needs.

God looked on His servant Paul imprisoned in Jerusalem, and He didn't just see
emotions. Paul was afraid. He needed
courage. Just like Philippians 4:19 said,
God literally met his need in Christ Jesus.
That day in Paul's prison cell, Christ stood
near and said, "Have courage!" He meant
"I'm right here. Take courage from Me!"
Paul's life could not be taken until the
mission was complete.

How desperate is your need for courage
right now? What are you facing that
cannot be dealt with by anything less
than God's gracious gift of motivation,
holy grit, and determination?

∽

*I am afflicted and needy; the Lord thinks
of me. You are my help and my deliverer.*
    —Psalm 40:17

Now I implore you, brothers, through the Lord Jesus Christ and through the love of the Spirit, to agonize together with me in your prayers to God on my behalf.
   —Romans 15:30

∽

The year I began working on my study of Paul, my heart was torn to pieces over a devastating loss. For several months no one outside our family and friends knew about it. Yet letters poured in from all over the nation saying something like this: "God has placed a heavy burden on my heart for Beth and her family. I do not know what is wrong, but I'm praying for them." I could hardly believe it.

I am absolutely certain those prayers delivered us from the pit of despair. Many times my soul would sink in grief. I'd feel like I was about to descend into depression. But each time I began to slip, I sensed something like a supernatural net disallowing me to descend another inch.

God can deliver anyone from anything at any time. He doesn't need any help. Yet He invites us to be part of His great work through prayer. I like to call this God's profit-sharing plan. When we pray for one another, we share the blessings when deliverance comes because we've been personally involved. Their thanksgiving becomes our thanksgiving.

∿

He has delivered us from such a terrible death, and He will deliver us; we have placed our hope in Him that He will deliver us again. And you can join in helping with prayer for us.
   —2 Corinthians 1:10–11

*Now as he spoke about righteousness,
self-control, and the judgment to come,
Felix became afraid and replied, "Leave for
now, but when I find time I'll call for you."*
   —Acts 24:25

∽

Confrontation with personal sin is never
convenient. Some of the messages I've
needed to hear most were those I wanted
to hear least. Like Felix, we in our human
natures often resist what is best for us.
But *unlike* Felix, we can dare to accept
the truth and find freedom.

While Felix felt fear, Luke tells us of no
reaction from Felix's wife, Drusilla. We
might surmise she was also convicted and
frightened, but I would offer a different
theory. Perhaps Drusilla simply did not
humble herself enough to be afraid.

She had quite an interesting heritage. Her father, Herod Agrippa I, bestowed on himself the glory due only to God. As a result he was eaten by worms and then died. Yet Drusilla led an adulterous life in spite of all she knew about morality and reverence for God. She willingly picked up the chain of pride and carried on.

God in His mercy reaches out to the immoral, ill-tempered, and boastful. Many hear but run the other way. Others hear but never apply. But some listen and are set free. God not only sent Felix and Drusilla a fitting message, He sent them a fitting messenger.

∽

Look, now is the acceptable time; look, now is the day of salvation.
   —2 Corinthians 6:2

They had some disagreements with him about
their own religion and about a certain Jesus,
a dead man whom Paul claimed to be alive.
　—Acts 25:19

∽

King Agrippa and his wife Bernice came
to Caesarea to pay respects to the new
governor, Festus, who told them about
Paul, and they decided to hear from the
apostle. As Paul had done with Felix and
Drusilla, he preached to the new trio.
Festus had been "at a loss" how to
investigate Paul's claims (v. 20).

I remember sharing with a loved one
how I know Christ is alive. He said, "I
believe in reincarnation," and, "I believe
a spiritual presence exists rather than a
certain God." He continued by repeating
the words "I believe" over and over.

Suddenly God gave me such a strange insight, and I was overwhelmed at the difference between my loved one and me. He believed the things he had been taught through New Age philosophy. I didn't just believe. I *knew*.

I gently said to him, "My God is not just Someone I believe in. He's Someone I know. I've felt His presence. I've seen His activity. I've experienced His deliverance. I've been touched by His healing. I've witnessed answered prayer. I've 'heard' Him speak straight to me through His Word. Yes, I believe. But more than that, I know."

∽

We are in the true One . . . in His Son Jesus Christ. He is the true God and eternal life.
—1 John 5:20

"I wish before God," replied Paul, *"that whether easily or with difficulty, not only you but all who listen to me today might become as I am—except for these chains."*
  —Acts 26:29

∽

I recently heard a famous actor share his testimony before a secular audience. He said when he was a boy, God revealed to him that he would reach out to thousands and thousands of people. All his life he had waited for God to call him to preach. Instead this young man developed into an Academy Award-winning actor.

He never knew what had happened to his calling. But on the night he was honored, he realized God had fulfilled the promise. The young boy never would have guessed how God would do what He said.

I wonder if Paul ever imagined his arrest would be the tool God would use to give him an all-expenses paid trip to his destination. God is the Deliverer, but we never know how He might deliver us. We see that God always fulfills His promises, just not always the way we imagine.

Praise God, He gives us what we need, not what we want. If Christ had come to immediately wear His crown, we would be hopelessly lost. A crown of thorns and a splintered cross had to precede a crown of jewels and a hallowed throne. If they hadn't, Christ would still have a throne but no earthly subjects to approach it.

∽

"Look, I am the LORD, the God of all flesh. Is anything too difficult for Me?"
   —Jeremiah 32:27

*Paul gave his advice and told them, "Men,
I can see that this voyage is headed toward
damage and heavy loss, not only of the cargo
and the ship, but also of our lives."*
  —Acts 27:9–10

∽

The ship's pilot and owner had insisted
on sailing regardless of difficulty. Like a
plot from a disaster movie, they put profit
above safety. They took advantage of the
first breeze and headed out, running a
risk that would eventually catch them
right between the eyes, driving them
helter-skelter on the open seas.

This particular peril in the apostle Paul's
life struck a chord in my heart for one
important reason: he and the others met
great difficulty because of someone else's
poor judgment.

I've gone through storms as a direct result of my own rebellion. I've also gone through storms as a result of spiritual warfare. Others were ordained directly by God for His glory. But sometimes the most difficult storms of all can be those that result from a wrong decision by a business partner, a boss, a driver, a jury, a teacher, a child, a spouse. These can have devastating repercussions on us.

We feel much greater potential for bitterness and unforgiveness when we have someone else to blame. If you find yourself in that position, keep your eyes (as Paul did) on God's greater purpose.

∽

Deliver me, my God, from the hand of the wicked, from the grasp of the unjust.
—Psalm 71:4

*For many days neither sun nor stars appeared,
and the severe storm kept raging; finally all
hope that we would be saved was disappearing.*
 —Acts 27:20

∽

Just when the passengers and crew
had lost hope, Paul stood to testify. He
told them, "This night an angel of the
God I belong to and serve stood by me,
saying, 'Don't be afraid, Paul. You must
stand before Caesar. And, look! God has
graciously given you all those who are
sailing with you'" (vv. 23–24).

God will probably not send an angel from
heaven to speak audibly to you, but He
may send a fellow believer, a neighbor,
a pastor, or friend. You can also hear Him
speak through His Word anytime you are
willing to open the Bible and receive.

The Old Testament character Job also suffered in ways we will never experience. I believe one reason he survived such tragedy was because God proved not to be silent as Job had feared. The place in which He spoke to Job is very applicable to us today. Job 40:6 tells us, "The LORD answered Job from the whirlwind."

God will speak to you too—straight to your heart. I can't promise that everything will be okay. It may be; it may not be. But I promise, based on the faithfulness of God, that *you* can be okay. Just don't pull up that anchor. And never let go of the rope.

∽

He reached down from on high and took hold of me; He pulled me out of deep waters.
    —Psalm 18:16

"I urge you to take some food. For this has to do with your survival, since not a hair will be lost from the head of any of you."
  —Acts 27:34

∾

God gave Paul an umbrella of protection to all on board the sinking ship because of Paul's obedience in ministry. Whether or not the others realized it, many were gathered in safety under his umbrella.

An attitude of obedience makes a difference both to the servant himself as well as to those close by. Servants of God can dramatically affect the lives of others positively or negatively. Under the prophet Jonah's umbrella, for example, many in the storm experienced calamity. Under Paul's umbrella, however, many found safety.

Is the sky rumbling? Are clouds darkening? Is a storm on the horizon? If you are a child of God, you will hold an umbrella in the storm, and you will not be under the umbrella alone. Neither will I. Our children will be under there with us. Our coworkers may be too. The flocks God has entrusted to us will be there. Even the lost are often drawn to people of faith when the winds begin to blow.

Child of God, you and I are centered on the bow of the ship when storms come and the waves crash. May the rest of the crew around us find an umbrella of blessing in our midst.

∽

He will give His angels orders concerning you,
to protect you in all your ways.
    —Psalm 91:11

*When the local people saw the creature
hanging from his hand, they said to one
another, "This man is probably a murderer,
and though he has escaped the sea, Justice
does not allow him to live!"*
    —Acts 28:4

∽

In all likelihood Paul picked up this
snake while he was gathering firewood.
When he put the branches in the fire, the
viper took the first way out: Paul's hand.

But God used it to reveal the beliefs of
the islanders. Although their assumption
was incorrect about Paul's guilt, their
statement revealed a limited knowledge
of the one true God. Although this island
had presumably never been evangelized,
its inhabitants had an awareness of a
divine judge who maintains "Justice."

Out of love for the world, God makes Himself known even in the most remote places on earth. Some call this element of self-disclosure "natural revelation." God desires for people to seek the unknown through the known, discovering a greater knowledge leading to salvation.

God is so merciful, isn't He? He doesn't just want people to be without excuse. He wants people not to be without a Savior. Justice was the natural light through which the people of Malta first perceived the one true God.

෴

From the creation of the world His invisible attributes, that is, His eternal power and divine nature, have been clearly seen, being understood through what He has made.
   —Romans 1:20

Paul went to him, and praying and laying his hands on him, he healed him. After this, the rest of those on the island who had diseases also came and were cured.

—Acts 28:8–9

∿

One detail of God's awesome, miraculous work on the island of Malta suggests that God was up to something spiritual: He enabled Paul to accomplish wholesale healing. All the sick were made well.

Sadly, an evangelist may not pack the house with good preaching and Spirit-filled worship, but he can draw large crowds with rumors of healing. Yes, God cares deeply about the sick, and He often heals physical illnesses, but seldom in Scripture did He use a servant to bring physical healing to an entire land.

God used the physical needs of those in Malta to draw attention to the only One who could meet their spiritual needs. He trusted Paul not to take credit for a work only God can do. We, too, must be careful to give God the glory when He uses us to accomplish things only He can do.

Think of a work He has accomplished through you. If you're uncomfortable with this request, you may still be taking too much credit. I'm asking you to boast in God, not in yourself. Pray about your availability for any work He might use you to accomplish. Then commit to give Him the glory.

∾

Not to us, Lord, not to us, but to Your name give glory because of Your faithful love.
    —Psalm 115:1

*There we found believers and were invited
to stay with them for seven days. And so we
came to Rome.*
    —Acts 28:14

∽

Paul had never seen anything like Rome.
At the time of his arrival, it was inhabited
by one million citizens and roughly the
same number of slaves. By even today's
standards, the city was gigantic.

As Paul approached this gargantuan city,
I believe God knew he would be overwhelmed by a great sea of strangers and
the certainty of enemies. Not coinciden-
tally, God met him at each stepping stone
to Rome with brothers. Keep in mind
that "brotherhood" in Christ refers to the
unique fellowship shared by brothers and
sisters in the faith.

Scripture refers to a natural sibling of Paul's only once, yet I counted ninety-nine times in his epistles when the apostle referred to other Christians as "brothers." As Paul approached Rome, God knew he needed everything this word entailed: "a fellowship of love" and "a community of life."

Paul's need was not unique. People are desperate for a sense of community today. We all want to feel like we belong. God recognizes our need, and He desires to meet our need through His church—the body of believers God organized to offer a community of life.

∽

Yes, brother, may I have joy from you in the Lord; refresh my heart in Christ.
    —Philemon 20

You are no longer foreigners and strangers,
but fellow citizens with the saints, and
members of God's household.
    —Ephesians 2:19

∽

In Paul's life, I see three strands that
formed the cord of brotherhood he felt
with other believers.

1. *Paul believed in the power of prayer and in*
our spiritual poverty without it. Over and
over in his letters, Paul assured churches
of his prayers. He didn't just ask God to
bless them. Paul jealously sought God's
best for them. He asked big things of God
because he knew God had big things to
give. Paul had experienced the riches of
an intimate relationship with Christ. He
wanted other believers to experience
those same riches.

2. *Paul believed that part of his calling was to share his gifts and faith with other Christians.* Believers have an obligation to one another as well as to the lost. My spiritual gifts were given for your edification; your spiritual gifts were given for mine.

3. *Paul desired to see all people come to Christ.* He preached to anyone who would listen, and he considered any convert a brother or sister. All were equally in need of salvation, and all equally loved by God.

As we imitate his approach to other believers, we will form cords of love not quickly broken.

∽

You are the body of Christ, and individual members of it.
   —*1 Corinthians 12:27*

Go to this people and say, "You will listen and listen, yet never understand; and you will look and look, yet never perceive."
—Acts 28:26

∽

If we continue resisting the further blessings and works of God in our lives, we may lose some ability to see past the obvious and the physical. Those who allow God to unleash His Holy Spirit in their lives are those who often perceive spiritual, eternal works in the physical and temporal realm.

I'll never forget the time Amanda's seat belt wouldn't fasten. Five years old at the time, she pushed and pushed on it to no avail, so I finally told her to crawl into the front seat. Seconds later, the window where she had been sitting inexplicably imploded and pieces of glass imbedded into the seat she had just left. "Thank You, dear God!" I exclaimed. She asked, "Do you really think that was God?" I said, "No, baby. I *know* that was God." Every now and then God blesses us with a good dose of perception. We not only see—we know!

When Paul tried to point out Christ's fulfillment of Old Testament prophecy, many Jews chose to close their eyes and refuse to see. God wants to give us supernatural sight. Let's not resist Him. Our lives are so much richer when we not only see but we also perceive!

∽

Their hearts are hard and insensitive, but I delight in Your instruction.
    —Psalm 119:70

*He stayed two whole years in his own rented
house. And he welcomed all who visited him,
proclaiming the kingdom of God and teaching
the things concerning the Lord Jesus Christ
with full boldness and without hindrance.*
   —Acts 28:30–31

∽

If someone asked, I'd tell them this is
what impresses me most about Paul:
his unparalleled passion for Christ
and his inconceivable perseverance.

When I was a child, someone gave my
brother an inflatable clown with sand in
the base. No matter how we socked that
clown, he always came back up for more.
The apostle was no clown, but every time
he got hit, he bounced back up for more.
Of course, the reason for his perseverance was his deep passion for Christ.

In Paul's life we get a glimpse of the risk we take when we put up our hand to God and say, "No more. I'm comfortable this way." We also realize how much we have to gain by remaining receptive to God. He has so much to give us.

You may never leave your native land or travel by sea, as Paul did. But if you love and serve God, your life will be a great adventure. He'll never take you anywhere He has not already prepared for your arrival. Keep trusting Him. There are more Acts to be performed.

∾

Let all who seek You rejoice and be glad in You; let those who love Your salvation continually say, "God is great!"
    —Psalm 70:4

I am saying this so that no one will deceive you with persuasive arguments.
  —Colossians 2:4

∾

Our world is replete with those who seek to control others through false and deceptive beliefs. Some of the "isms" in play during Paul's day included:

1. *Gnosticism.* The word *gnosis* means "knowledge." Followers of the gnostic belief system believed that knowledge, rather than faith, led to salvation.

2. *Legalism.* Paul exposed the fruitlessness of keeping endless laws that condemn rather than liberate the believer to pursue godliness. Only a love relationship with Christ can change the human heart and bring about genuine piety.

3. *Mysticism.* This is the belief that we can obtain direct knowledge of God from our thoughts, feelings, or experiences. Biblical faith declares Jesus Christ to be the source of our knowledge about God.

4. *Asceticism.* Followers of asceticism do not stop at the wise denial of dangerous, perverse, or unhealthy practices but rather deny the body unnecessarily in an attempt to force it into submission.

We still battle many of the same philosophies faced by the early believers. Though the list of "isms" may change, Satan is still up to the same old tricks.

∽

Do not believe every spirit, but test the spirits to determine if they are from God.
  —1 John 4:1

*Be careful that no one takes you captive
through philosophy and empty deceit based
on human tradition.*
    —Colossians 2:8

∽

The best way for a child of God to avoid
being kidnapped by false teaching is to
stay close to home. Children in natural
families cannot live their entire lives in
their yards, but children in the spiritual
family of God can! Continuing to live in
Christ means remaining close to Him
and retaining a focus on Him. Any other
focus can lead to deceptive doctrine, even
if the focus is a biblical concept.

Many of us have probably let something
temporarily become a greater focus than
Christ Himself. I've seen a specific belief
or detail of doctrine become such a focus.

Remember, any doctrine that loses connection with the Head has been twisted into deception. We are less likely to be kidnapped when we stay close to home by staying focused on the Head, Jesus Christ.

Spiritually, we have difficulty growing up until we've grown down. We form deep roots by knowing the basics of our faith. We can receive Christ and be enthusiastic and still fall into confusion the first time someone confronts us with strange doctrine. Our roots are our basics. They keep us from being easy targets.

∾

Then we will no longer be little children, tossed by the waves and blown around by every wind of teaching.
    —*Ephesians 4:14*

*Wives, submit to your own husbands as to the
Lord, for the husband is head of the wife as
also Christ is head of the church.*
  —Ephesians 5:22–23

∽

The attitude of all Christians is to be
submissive to one another. No discussion
of this topic can stay on track apart from
that spirit. Paul's primary directive to
women dealt with submission, while his
primary directive to men dealt with love.
Could it be that he was targeting the areas
most likely to be our weaknesses?

Here's what submission does *not* mean:
It does not mean women are under the
authority of men in general. It does not
mean inequality. It does not mean wives
should treat their husbands like God.
It does not mean slavery.

Two realizations have changed my entire
attitude on this subject:

1. *God is good and loving.* He would never
give approval to meanness or abuse. Any
misuse of submission by either the
husband or wife is sin.

2. *God granted women a measure of freedom
in submission that we can learn to enjoy.*
It is a relief to know that as a wife and
mother, I am not totally responsible for
my family. I have a husband to look to for
counsel and direction. Paul regarded
husbands and wives as spiritual equals
with functional differences.

∽

*We must pursue what promotes peace and
what builds up one another.*
   —Romans 14:19

Husbands, love your wives, just as also Christ loved the church and gave Himself for her.
  —Ephesians 5:25

∽

For a society where women were little more than property, passed from father to husband, this command for men to love their wives was a radical idea. Paul knew that few role models existed for the men to follow. He gave them the best role model possible: Jesus Christ.

1. *Husbands should love their wives sacrificially.* Just as a husband must be careful not to abuse his wife's exhortation to submission, a wife must not abuse her husband's exhortation to sacrifice. Some men work several jobs sacrificing time at home in a continual effort to raise the standard of living for their families.

2. *Husbands should love their wives in ways that encourage purity.* Christ encourages purity in His bride, the church. God calls upon husbands to treat their wives as pure vessels even in physical intimacy.

3. *Husbands should "love their wives as their own bodies" (v. 28).* I wonder if Paul might have been thinking, "If you love yourself at all, mister, then love your wife because life will be far more pleasant under the same roof with a well-loved woman!"

Marriage is like a three-legged stool—a submissive wife, a loving husband, and Christ. All three must be in place.

∽

If I give my body to be burned, but do not have love, I gain nothing.
　　—1 Corinthians 13:3

Finally, be strengthened by the Lord and by His vast strength.
—Ephesians 6:10

∽

Our victory is sure, but the fight will be difficult. Hear your Commander as He exhorts you to do the following:

1. *Realize your natural limitations.* We cannot enjoy spiritual victory without calling on the power of God. We are only strong when we are "strengthened by the Lord and by His vast strength."

2. *Remember the "full armor" (v. 11).* After at least six thousand years of practice on human targets, your enemy won't waste arrows on well-armed places. He will aim for the spots you and I leave uncovered. I know it from experience.

3. *Recognize your real enemies.* The struggle of warfare does not originate in spouses, in-laws, neighbors, coworkers, or any earthly foe. Spiritual forces of evil exist. Not every problem we have is warfare, of course. Sometimes we need to repent from sin. Other times, however, we must fortify against the evil one.

4. *Realize our enemies' limitations.* Satan and his powers and principalities cannot do anything they want with us. Walk in the freedom of knowing that when you received Christ, God dropped His Holy Spirit into you, slammed on the lid, and tightened the cap. Nothing can get in.

∽

They confronted me in the day of my distress, but the LORD was my support.
—Psalm 18:18

*Put on the full armor of God so that you can
stand against the tactics of the Devil.*
　—Ephesians 6:11

∽

You've likely studied this list of weaponry
before, but let's continue to learn while
we live, and fight while we have strength.

The *belt of truth* represents not living a lie
in any part of our lives, living free of
secret areas of hypocrisy.

The *breastplate of righteousness* is the
protection we receive when we choose
the right thing even when we feel like
choosing the wrong thing.

Feet readied with the gospel of peace. We can
remain balanced because, though we're at
war with Satan, we're at peace with God.

The *shield of faith* is our protection when Satan tempts us to disbelieve God. We're not called to have faith in our faith but to have faith in God and never doubt Him.

The *helmet of salvation* protects our minds. Continue to fill it with the Word of God and things pertaining to godliness.

The *sword of the Spirit* is our only offensive weapon against the evil one. Know and use the Word of God persistently!

We can do nothing to change the fact that warfare is a reality. We can, however, decide whether to be victims or victors.

∽

Fight the good fight for the faith; take hold of eternal life, to which you were called.
—1 Timothy 6:12

I, Paul, as an elderly man and now also as a prisoner of Christ Jesus, appeal to you for my child, whom I fathered while in chains—Onesimus.
    —Philemon 9–10

∾

In the last years of the apostle's life, four of his five biblical letters were written to individuals rather than to bodies of believers. One of these was addressed to Philemon, a believer from Colosse whom Paul probably met while ministering in a nearby city. Quite possibly Paul had been the one who had personally introduced Philemon to the Savior.

They developed a friendship, and Paul saw Philemon become an active worker for the gospel. Philemon must have been a wealthy man as well as a slave owner.

During the intervening years, one of
these slaves—Onesimus—had run away,
apparently stealing from Philemon in the
process. And by the providence of God,
he had found himself in Rome, where he
met Paul. Perhaps while on the run, he
had stolen again and been incarcerated
with Paul. Either way, imagine their
meeting when they realized they both
knew Philemon.

You can be sure their meeting wasn't
a coincidence. God had ordained the
fugitive slave to have a heart-to-heart
collision with the most well-known
slave of grace in all Christendom.

∿

Restore us, Lord God of Hosts; look on us with
favor, and we will be saved.
　　—Psalm 80:19

*Perhaps this is why he was separated from
you for a brief time, so that you might get him
back permanently, no longer as a slave, but
more than a slave—as a dearly loved brother.*
—Philemon 15–16

∽

Paul did more than preach to people. He
lived the concepts he taught. When he
met the slave Onesimus, he saw a man in
need of a Savior. Paul didn't just preach to
him about the mercy of God, he showed
it to him. He took Onesimus's debt not
only out of justice but also out of mercy,
because a sinner needed grace. Paul
wanted Philemon to show mercy as well.

The closer we draw near to God and the
more we behold His majesty, the more
we relate to the psalmist who said, "What
is man that You remember him?" (Ps. 8:4).

Paul recognized the pit from which
God had pulled him. He knew it was
grace that had bridged the wide gulf fixed
between them. His proposal for restora-
tion between Philemon and Onesimus
required both men to walk humbly. Paul,
for his part, had to humble himself by not
ordering Philemon to do what he ought
to do based on any past obligations. He
appealed to him on the basis of love.

When God sent His Son to be an atoning
sacrifice for our sins, He fulfilled the law
with love and mercy. Paul's proposal was
to let mercy reign.

∽

*Be restored, be encouraged, be of the same
mind, be at peace, and the God of love and
peace will be with you.*
    —2 Corinthians 13:11

Finally brothers, whatever is true, whatever is honorable, whatever is just, whatever is pure, whatever is lovely, whatever is commendable—if there is any moral excellence and if there is any praise—dwell on these things.
  —Philippians 4:8

෨

Proverbs 23:7 describes man with the words, "For as he thinks within himself, so he is." We might say a person feels like he or she thinks. Our human natures tend toward negative and destructive thoughts. If ten people complimented you today and one person criticized, which would you go to bed thinking about tonight? Probably the criticism!

Destructive, negative thinking is a habit that can be broken, but this thief takes diligence to overcome. God knows the tendency of the mind to think and rethink on a certain subject, meditating on things. Paul gave us a wonderful checklist for determining whether our thoughts are worth thinking: whatever is true, honorable, just, pure, lovely, commendable . . . "dwell on these things."

I struggle with destructive thinking, just like you do. God has used Scripture memory and Bible study to set me free. I continue to make His Word a daily priority, but He also blesses the refreshment I gain from other wholesome, uplifting alternatives. Worthy thought patterns are a key to contentment.

~

A discerning mind seeks knowledge, but the mouth of fools feeds on foolishness.
   —Proverbs 15:14

*He considered me faithful . . . one who was
formerly a blasphemer, a persecutor, and an
arrogant man.*
    —1 Timothy 1:12—13

༄

God used Paul to perform more wonders
and to birth more churches than any
other human in the New Testament. In
a quarter of a century, Paul had plenty of
time to forget who he had been, taking
pride in his powerful ministry.

One reason God leaves our memories
of past repented sin intact is because a
twinge of memory is indeed profitable to
us. Pride is the archenemy of ministry.
I think one reason Paul continued to
remember who he had been was because
his love for Christ continued to grow.
The more he loved Christ, the more he

wondered how he could have sinned against Him so horrendously in his past. I've personally experienced this. Even though I know I am fully forgiven, the deeper my love for Christ has grown, the more I regret past sins.

In his final letter to Timothy, Paul would write, "Nevertheless, God's solid foundation stands firm, having this inscription: 'The Lord knows those who are His'" (2 Tim. 2:19). We are wise never to forget who we were. Never forgetting who we were lends a far greater appreciation for who we now are!

∽

Remember that you were a slave in the land of Egypt, and the LORD your God brought you out of there with a strong hand.
    —Deuteronomy 5:15

*A woman should learn in silence with full
submission. I do not allow a woman to teach
or to have authority over a man.*
   —1 Timothy 2:11–12

～

Glancing through the book of 1 Timothy,
you'll notice a continuing exhortation for
order in the churches. In stressing this,
Paul made some statements about women
that raise controversy. Although he used
far more ink to address deacons and
overseers, I don't want to be charged with
cowardice by omitting any mention of
his instructions to women.

The Christian movement was new and
fragile. Any taint of adverse publicity
could greatly hinder the mission of
the church and mean persecution for
believers. Women had to restrain

their new freedom in Christ (Gal. 3:28) so as not to impede the progress of the gospel. Paul's "weaker brother" principle applies, where he said, "Be careful that this right of yours in no way becomes a stumbling block to the weak" (1 Cor. 8:9). Thus, women were to learn quietly, without calling attention to themselves.

We cannot regard verses 11 and 12 as a prohibition against women opening their mouths in church or men learning anything biblical from women. Paul issued differing instructions for churches based on their cultural settings and his desire for order in the church.

∽

I am with you in spirit, rejoicing to see your good order and the strength of your faith.
   —Colossians 2:5

*Practice these things; be committed to them,
so that your progress may be evident to all.*
    —1 Timothy 4:15

∽

Paul's exhortations to Timothy stand as
timeless words of advice to every servant
of the living God, regardless of generation or gender. I'd like to look at a few of
these today, a few more tomorrow.

1. *"Train yourself in godliness"* (v. 7).
Salvation is a gift; godliness is a pursuit.
The word meaning "to train" is *gumnazo*,
from which we derive our English word
"gymnasium." The apostle drew a parallel
between an athlete preparing for the
Greek games and a believer pursuing
godliness. An athlete who is preparing
for intense competition makes frequent
visits to the gym.

2. *"Be an example"* (*v. 12*). God is practical.
His Word works. He wants us to be living
proof by our example. If we are trying to
lead others but are not closely following
Christ, we are misleading.

3. *"Do not neglect the gift that is in you"*
(*v. 14*). When we receive Christ, God
gives us spiritual gifts, but they must then
be developed, cared for, and cultivated.
God directs us to fan into flame the gifts
He has given us. He honors a beautiful
blend of gift and grit! He gives the gift,
then He expects us to have the grit to
learn how to use it effectively.

∽

Be diligent to present yourself approved to God,
a worker who doesn't need to be ashamed,
correctly teaching the word of truth.
  —2 Timothy 2:15

Good works are obvious, and those that are not obvious cannot remain hidden.
—*1 Timothy 5:25*

〜

Today we consider two other imperatives that were part of Paul's instruction to Timothy, his son in the faith.

1. "*Keep yourself pure*" (5:22). Nothing has the potential to destroy ministries and testimonies like impurity. Paul told Timothy to stand as a guard over purity in his own life. I must take responsibility for purity in my life; you must take responsibility for purity in your life. If you are trying to keep yourself pure but you continue to fall, I encourage you to seek godly counsel. It is not too late to consecrate your life to God and find the victory He has accomplished for you.

2. Avoid *"irreverent, empty speech"* (6:20). As believers in Christ, we are sacred temples of His Holy Spirit. We have a choice as to what crosses the threshold and finds a place in our temples. Paul exhorts believers to discern a line in conversation that should not be crossed.

I pray that Paul's life compels you to be an active part of God's agenda, eager for your life to leave footprints someone else can follow straight to Christ. None of this happens accidentally. Godliness and effective ministry take attention, but nothing you could pour your energies into will ever have a greater payoff.

∽

Everyone who has this hope in Him purifies himself just as He is pure.
—1 John 3:3

Older women are to be reverent in behavior, not slanderers, not addicted to much wine. They are to teach what is good.

—Titus 2:3

∽

If you are fortunate to have benefited from some godly mentors, you know that none of them were in your life accidentally. Paul, in his charge to older women, points out certain qualifications for a mentor to younger women.

1. *Reverent in the way she lives.* Her actions are to be those identifying her as one who respects God. Each of the women who have mentored me were quite different in personality, but they all shared one common denominator: their lives were replete with a reverence for God. Those I respect most are those who respect God.

2. Not slanderous. Slanderous people thrive on conflict and division. The godly mentor sets an example by edifying others through her speech—rejoicing over their victories and hurting with them in defeat.

3. Not addicted to much wine. Today we could fill a grocery aisle with potentially enslaving substances. Godly women avoid turning to harmful remedies when they are feeling desperate or vulnerable.

Older women are to teach younger women about genuine beauty: God's idea of a beautiful woman.

∾

Without guidance, people fall, but with many counselors there is deliverance.
   —Proverbs 11:14

Encourage the young women to love their husbands and children, to be sensible, pure, good homemakers, and submissive to their husbands, so that God's message will not be slandered.

   —Titus 2:4–5

∾

Paul mentions three distinct ways in which older women are to help younger women. Let's see what we can learn.

1. *Love your husband.* The original word used for "love" in this verse is *philandros*, which speaks of loving someone as a friend. By our feminine natures, women don't often share the same interests as men. But we can *learn* to share their interests! I want to be a better friend to my husband. If you're married, let's make this commitment together.

2. *Love your children.* You may be thinking, "Who needs to be taught how to love her children?" Lots of wounded people, that's who. Hug your children often and tell them you love them, whether these actions come easily for you or not.

3. *Be busy at home.* Homes and families do not take care of themselves. Children don't raise themselves. A marriage doesn't improve itself. Someone has to watch over it to encourage growth and intimacy. The wife and mother has something to give her home and family that no one else can supply as effectively: tenderness, nurturing, a personal touch.

∽

I will pay attention to the way of integrity. . . .
I will live with integrity of heart in my house.
    —Psalm 101:2

*I am not ashamed, because I know whom I
have believed and am persuaded that He is
able to guard what has been entrusted to me
until that day.*
    —2 Timothy 1:12

∽

A person confined and facing death
inevitably turns the mental pages of
the past. Surely Paul was no different.
He must have thought about Tarsus—
his mother's face, his father's voice, his
childhood in a Jewish community.

He must have recalled the classroom
debates he enjoyed, the way people
whispered about his genius behind his
back, his drive to persecute the people of
the Way, the blinding light that sent him
to his knees. He traded respect and honor
for a life of rejection and tribulation.

If his childhood friends could have seen him in that horrendous dungeon, they might have surmised that he had traded everything for nothing. What do you have when you have nothing left? You only have what you know. Faced with humiliation, Paul's sanity was protected by his certainty. He knew the One in whom he had believed.

As the chains gripped his hands and feet and the stench of death assailed him, he recalled everything he had entrusted to his Savior. With chained hands, Paul could still touch the face of God.

∽

For this I suffer, to the point of being
bound like a criminal; but God's message
is not bound.
    —2 Timothy 2:9

For me, living is Christ and dying is gain.
    —Philippians 1:21

∽

Our entire journey together has been an effort to see the heart of a man who could sincerely make such a statement. Christ had profoundly transformed Paul's attitude toward life and death.

1. *Paul saw death as a departure.* His whole life was a series of departures. He had followed the leading of the Spirit to city after city, never knowing what awaited him as he entered. But one result was inevitable—as surely as he arrived, he would depart. To him, settling in would have been pointless until then. Paul had faithfully done his time in Rome and, predictably, another departure awaited him. This time, he was going home.

2. *Paul saw death as a rescue.* God certainly rescued Paul many times on this earth, just as He has rescued us, yet Paul knew the greatest rescue of all awaited him.

3. *Paul saw death as a safe passage.* Recall the words of 2 Timothy 4:18. God will not only rescue us "from every evil work" but will bring us "safely into His heavenly kingdom." God is not simply trying to snatch us from danger. He desires to draw us to Himself spiritually, then one day physically. When our ultimate rescue comes, God's purpose is to deliver us to Himself—safely.

∽

"If I go away and prepare a place for you,
I will come back and receive you to Myself,
so that where I am you may be also."
    —John 14:3

I have fought the good fight, I have finished the race, I have kept the faith.
    —2 Timothy 4:7

∾

Paul once wrote, "Now I know in part, but then I will know fully, as I am fully known" (1 Cor. 13:12). The partial knowledge of Christ that Paul had acquired in his lifetime was the same knowledge he claimed to be worth every loss (see Phil. 3:8–10).

Oh, my friend, if partial knowledge of the Lord Jesus is worth every loss, what then will full knowledge be like? I cry out with our brother Paul, "Oh, the depth of the riches both of the wisdom and the knowledge of God!" (Rom. 11:33). One day the prayer of the apostle will be answered for all of us.

Until then, may God find us faithful, waiting to hang our hats on heaven's door. "For I am persuaded that neither death nor life, nor angels nor rulers, nor things present, nor things to come, nor powers, nor height, nor depth, nor any other created thing will have the power to separate us from the love of God that is in Christ Jesus our Lord!" (Rom. 8:38–39).

Most Worthy Lord,
make me a drink offering
and take me not home
until the cup is overturned
the glass broken
and every drop loosed
for Your glory.

﹏

Your labor in the Lord is not in vain.
  —1 Corinthians 15:58

TAKE ONE DAY AT A TIME
AND SEE WHAT HAPPENS.

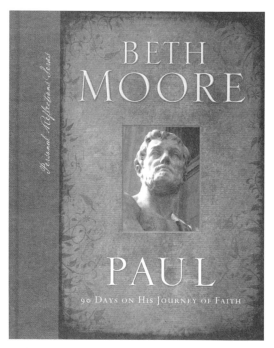

Paul: 90 Days on His Journey of Faith | **AVAILABLE NOW**
978-0-8054-4934-1 | $24.99

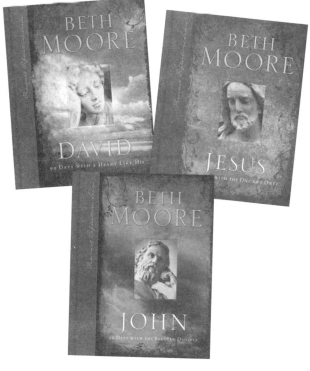

GREAT DAY BY DAY BOOKS
FROM BETH MOORE

Believing God Day by Day
978-0-8054-4798-9 | $14.99

Breaking Free Day by Day
978-0-8054-4646-3 | $14.99

Praying God's Word Day by Day
978-0-8054-4420-9 | $14.99